Fun with Dad

By Warren Bright

Library For All Ltd.

Fun with Dad

I'm Mahlee and I can't wait to go kick the footy with Dad today.

3

It's my favourite thing to do, rain or shine.

Smiling, I ask Dad, "Are we going to the oval today?"

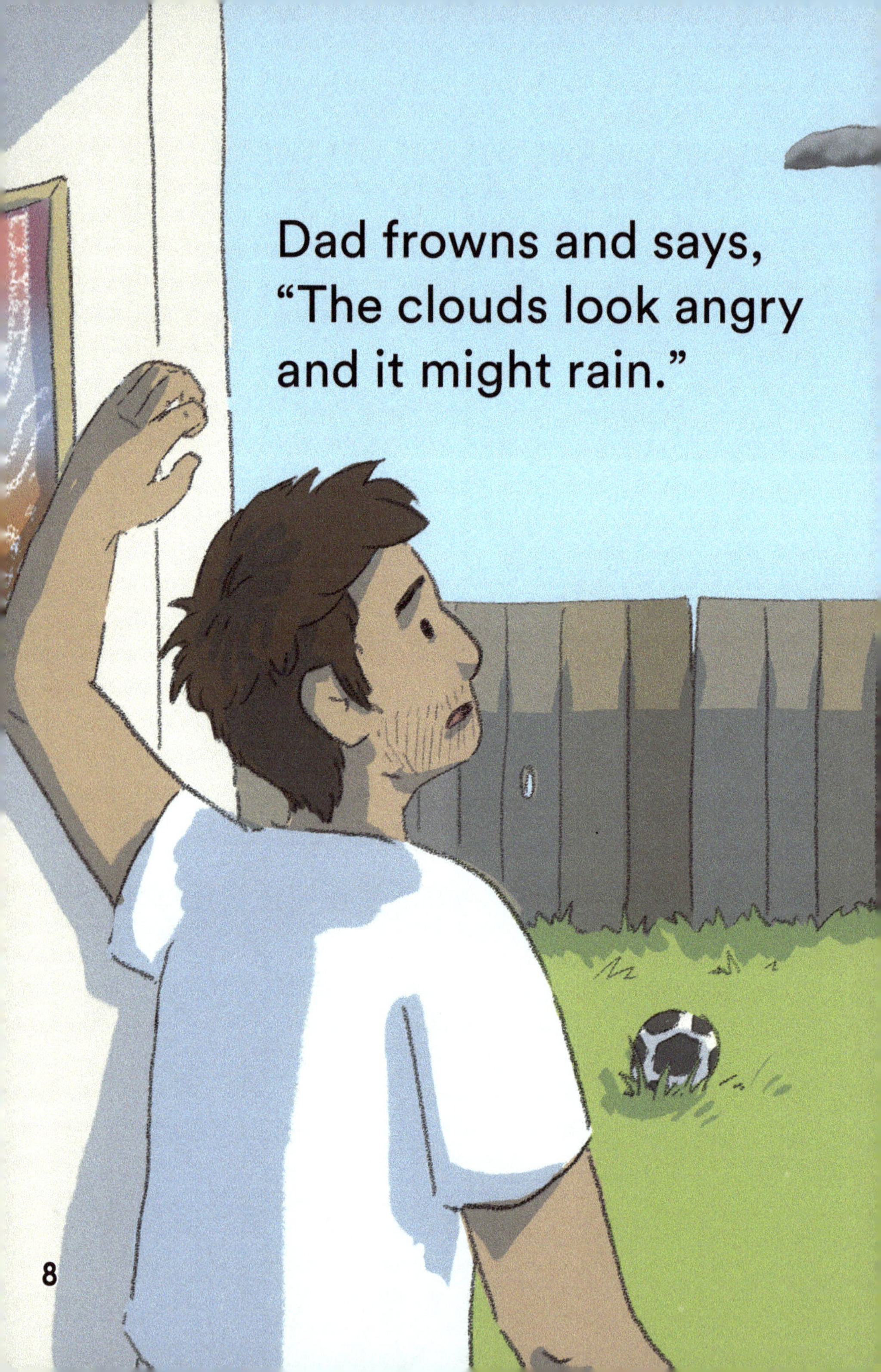

Dad frowns and says,
"The clouds look angry
and it might rain."

My smile fades.

I hope the clouds go away.

Dad smiles and says, "Let's go anyway, Mahlee. Getting a little wet is okay."

I grab my football and we both walk to the oval.

The sun shines through the clouds as we kick the ball for ages.

Just as we get back home, the clouds burst open with a big rainstorm.

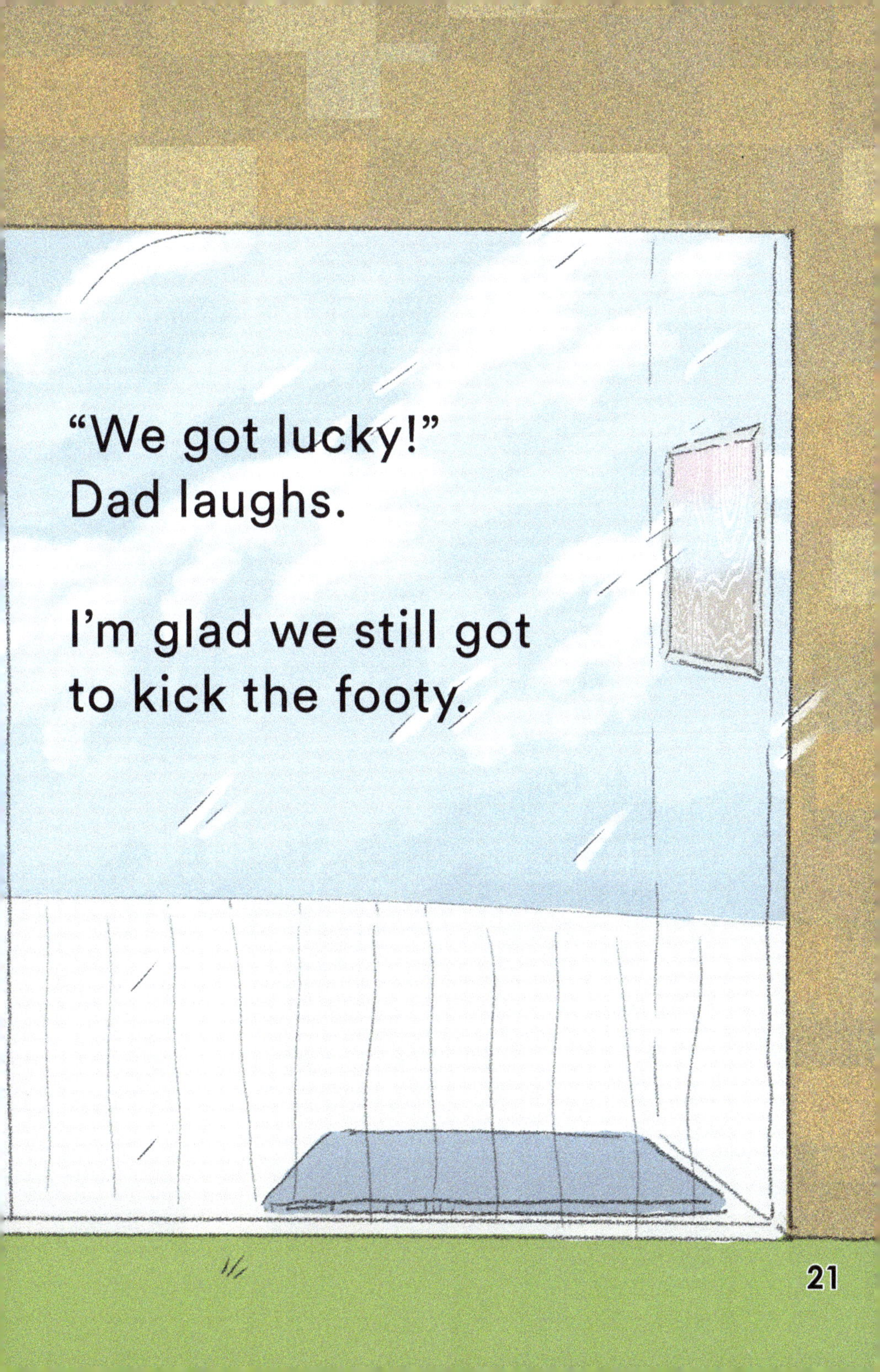

“We got lucky!”
Dad laughs.

I’m glad we still got
to kick the footy.

You can use these questions to talk about this book with your family, friends and teachers.

What did you learn from this book?

Describe this book in one word. Funny? Scary? Colourful? Interesting?

How did this book make you feel when you finished reading it?

What was your favourite part of this book?

download our reader app
getlibraryforall.org

About the author

Warren is a Wiradjuri man born in Narrandera and lives in Canberra. He loves catching up with family and telling stories. His favourite story is *The Rainbow Serpent*.

Darwin

NORTHERN
TERRITORY

QUEENSLAND

WESTERN
AUSTRALIA

SOUTH
AUSTRALIA

Brisbane

NEW SOUTH
WALES

Perth

Adelaide

Sydney

ACT
Canberra

VICTORIA
Melbourne

Author's Country

TASMANIA
Hobart

Our Yarning

Want to discover more books from this collection? Our Yarning is a collection of books written by Aboriginal and Torres Strait Islander peoples across Australia.

We know that children learn better, and enjoy reading more, when they see themselves in the stories, characters and illustrations of the books they read.

To download the app, visit the Google Play Store on any Android device and search 'Our Yarning'.

www.ingramcontent.com/pod-product-compliance
Lightning Source LLC
Chambersburg PA
CBHW042344040426
42448CB00019B/3400